Dead Moments' Thoughts

Samantha Jane Calanog

Presentation by *BookLeaf Publishing*

Web: www.bookleafpub.com

E-mail: info@bookleafpub.com

ISBN: 9789357441957

First edition 2023

This book, I dedicate to..

YOU

because, why not?

*Whoever says or makes you feel that you
don't deserve one,*

even if it was your own voice,

*let this be the first of the many others that
I'll aspire to keep coming.*

Because you're worth it!

ACKNOWLEDGEMENT

This book would like to acknowledge each one of you who unhesitatingly purchased this book-for-a-cause. "ALL" the proceeds from this book sale will go to charity. That probably makes this one of the best purchases you've made. Thank you!

PREFACE

This book wouldn't be in your hands had it not been for God who blessed me with the privilege to have my work published. I thought, how cool is that to flip the pages of my work, the work that renders the purpose of my pain. I've always romanticized about my feelings and every realization from the hardships I went through, which in the end, just helped me learn more about myself and the big God who reveals himself through those hardships. To my proofreaders, you've been awesome! Hyrum, Karen, MJ, huge thanks to you guys! To every soul who gave meaning to my experiences, you know who you are, all of you have colored my world in a way that still came out beautiful, poetic even. Xxx

Trust and People

It's warming when people trusts you.
Trust, it's intoxicating!

You know well enough there were times that you
struggle yourself,
in trusting your self, no matter how
incontestable you feel of being trustworthy.

It was hard work. It's broken some hearts,
shattered some dreams
and disappointed some people who didn't
deserve someone insubstantial trust-wise.

Trust that's been broken in the past, I could only
wish I can repair.
But God blessed me with a now.

And if tomorrow will be another now,
it'll be another day I'll make certain no trust gets
wasted away.
No, never again.

The Bigger Person

You paint faces with the biggest smiles,
faces that never knew your pain
and how you sulk in the dark recesses
of your heart where hurt remains

Your fascination in lending a hand
amplifies the compassionate you
by a thousand folds, that one can say
you are too good to be true

You don't always make the best of choices
but you're a well intentioned soul,
you explore loose ends and loop holes
though it's your happiness that it stole

I hope one day someone could appease
the parts of you that drench in gloom,
I hope he makes you laugh as hard
that it echoes in a room

I pray that you find a love so pure
that it makes sadness inconceivable
and your entire day's work worth it,
it's everything you deserve after all

I pray that he salves your brokenness,
bring back the joy you give away
and make you believe that happy endings
do happen come what may

A Fairytale

She's a princess whose boldness and hopeless
romanticness breathes life to the prince others
believe to be non-existent.

She fearlessly plays her chances for that love,
for him.

And, I can't help but admire how she
audaciously rolled up her sleeves to feel it in her
skin.

The warmth and comfort of his touch,
aware of all the uncertainties, aware of the risks,
the risk of it being the touch of death,
the spindle that will bring her to a forever of
deep sleep
or the touch that will finally bring all her aches
to a fairytale end.

Deceitful Heart

I'm sat on the fence about calling out to you,
to be comforted for one of the many "one last
times" I swore to myself I will ever have.

Your hug, it's safety, it's home, and it displeases
me how it makes my heart long for more.

Hearts can be deceiving!
It wants one thing,
that seemingly vital thing,
only to reveal itself to be the very thing that
breaks it.

And when it can't get what it wants, it breaks
some more.
It screeches with pain and it's deafening.

And it could only wish it's cry is loud enough for
you to hear. Loud enough, in spite its struggle to
triumph over all the forces
that tries to box and silence it.

Fruits of Labour

Don't give her excuses. Give her your brutal
truths.

She laid her heart on the table, bare, vulnerable,
unarmed.
For once, just this once! Show her you're
someone who's willing to do the same.

She deserves to know the bits she needed to
guard her heart from.

And if you love her, you'll hammer into your
head, utterly everything it takes
to bring her walls down.

But if you truly, sincerely love her, once those
walls are down,
you make sure you shield her, that you defend
her and nourish her.

From there you'll see,
her branches will grow again,
her flowers will bloom and all who believed she
won't endure will wonder,

where's this earth she's now flourishing in? and
who's relishing her fruits?

your fruits of labour.

She's Set Free

There's a lot she runs away from,
people she avoided, places she'd bow her head
down as she walk past,
moments she won't stay in, songs she skipped,
things she won't touch, just like how she refused
parts of her to be touched.

She was cautious, a little smarter and almost
always healing.

Then she tripped, again.
You'd think it's something she should have been
used to by now.
But once again, she bled, as she picked the
shards of herself.

Then she smiled, because as she was putting
them back together,
she saw parts of her that she has never seen
before
and didn't knew of until the pieces of her are all
over the place.

Now, she knows what she's made of.
She knows herself better now.

She now knows who and what she's always
meant to be, no longer hiding from the shadows
of what the world needs her to be.
She's set free!

Ode to My Heart

Up to this day you showed beyond doubt
to be the sturdiest part of me,
God molded you to feel for people
who'd often prove themselves unworthy

You try to see the best in everyone
although it takes a toll on you
and even when the world questions your aim,
you still beat like you never knew

Of the promises, false hope and lies
those unsparing souls made you to believe
and languish in agony every night
then creeps for whatever's left it can thieve

When the brain screams "You're Irrational!"
you say, "Nothing's ever too much",
that you'll never cease in seeking out
to find another heart to touch

Oh my dear heart how you amaze me!
How you make me so full of pride!
Your gift of love maybe undermined
but you remain as my best guide

You're what makes me every inch deserving,
you resilient, you selfless, you,
what a pleasure it would be to the one
who you'd gift your lifetime to.

Beauty in Goodbyes

Who said goodbyes can't be beautiful?
The longing, it can be a terrifying thing.

But a truly loving heart will yearn more for the
happiness of the other,
even in the midst of uncertainty that whatever's
left will stay the same until that person comes
back,
IF that person comes back at all.

We can't always cling to the odds that goodbye
could mean "see you later".
You see, that's the beauty in goodbyes.

If it meant farewell, it leaves you with an
exquisite story to tell.
A story that took but also makes a part of you.
A story that will try and fill the crevice in your
heart.

It doesn't make it whole again but it holds it
together, so that despite the crack,
the heart does not break.

Coexistence

She's not her without it. It's the pea under the
huge pile of mattress
and if you're the one, you'll feel it, you'll feel
her,
the part of her that craves to let loose, go crazy,
run wild!

But she knows no one takes better care of
herself, better than herself,
so as hard as it is, she tames her wild horses
down, pressing it to patiently wait.

She's got great faith in God. She hangs on to
that. "He will come" she tells it.
The right one. The one with the prerogative to
speak to the parts of her
that longs to be loved wild and longs to love him
more wildly back.
The parts of her that sits beneath her refined
demeanor, they coexist.

And man you'll be the luckiest when she allows
it to flood on you,
coz she ain't holding anything back.

She's saved the best of herself for you and I
plead of you,
appreciate that!

You Didn't Choose Her

You didn't choose her, she made you choose her.
Like a moth to a flame. She's got that in her!
And you're just scared to admit it.

That doesn't make you a weakling. But even
when you think it does,
she knows exactly how it feels to be weak,
and you, just feeling, and acknowledging that
feeling, to her, is strength.

You don't know, how much she wants to know,
that you're more human than she thought.

Sometimes, to win, you got to lose. But, what's
actually there to lose?
You're definitely not losing yourself. If anything,
you're losing your pride and ego.

Flow with her. She may be the kind that needs
protecting,
but she knows damn well that your heart needs
protecting too,
and you can count on her for that.

Good Nights

The night, to her, is a lot of things,
it's when she shreds dead weight from her skin
of what every single soul presumes of her,
but none of which is her from within

The dark of the night used to scare her
now she lets it keep her company,
allowing it to wrap around her each night
to help her at least rest easily

After all her pains presses her to be
every person she needed in her life
a confidant, a true friend, the list is endless
that in the end just provokes a strife

Of who to be and when to be it
each time she doesn't feel enough,
and the night is the only time when she
can do away with staying tough

The night, to her, tickles a lot of feelings
she's too busy to mind during the day,
so the night leaves her with the serenity
to help her decide which ones she'll let stay

The night is her secret hiding place
and the moment she won't cease to remember,
that when all else was wearing her down
the night have always been good to her.

Another Stranger

It's tempting, but don't!   Please don't introduce
him to another stranger.
Be true to your core. Don't allow anyone to
change that!

If you lose him for being you, that's alright. It
may not feel alright, but let it be alright!
You owe that to yourself!

Be your own, love your own my dear.
Cut and burn the string that gives people a hold
over you.
Detest undue influence. Would you rather lose
yourself?

So please, let him see you,
be no one else but you
and not another stranger.

Just a little boy

She thought you were different. When you
strode along in your crisp tuxedo,
she didn't realize you were just a little boy.
And now she's watching that little boy take his
sneaky steps back.

You tricked her, when you tried to take shape as
someone who's got his thing together, when truth
is, you're just like the others.

The others who happily takes, but will never
want to be obliged to care for anything,
no matter how precious, if it is fragile.

I tell you, her kind is rare and practically extinct.
In a world full of wastelands and sink holes, she
took her time to become
a safe dwelling place.

You all crave for adventure, that you don't take
enough time to discern
what shells are for keeps and what's worth
throwing back to the sea.

You either grow up now or travel the entire
world, only to rush back to her,
and wish that, it's not yet late, that you've not
come too late.

Ruins

All that's left of her are ruins
that enlightens all she has survived,
the repositories of the past life
she no longer feels the need to hide

All her life she defended warped truth
that became the death of her,
frowning upon the upright and just
and disgracefully finding joy in blunder

Constantly feeding the needs of the flesh
and hearts that are filled with greed,
she got sickened with the ways of the world
that it made sense to take heed

Of the deception in the society
she no longer wants to belong in
when it's easier for many to unite with the
madness
solely, she chose to duly begin

To seek the truth in the ways of the Lord
and grow appetite for the world of grace,
despise the callous disregard for destruction
that kept advancing in a fast pace

Her preserved ruins now shines hope
to those still walking in the dark,
reaching out to every soul she can spare
from what can only leave them with grave mark

His Hope

Oh how she craves to play her piano and sing
her heart out
to another soul who would listen closely, not just
to the sound it makes
but to the music from her heart.

She earnestly wishes he'd realize, that every
word that would fall off her lips
were intended to reach right through him,

Wrap his delicate heart around so that he feels
safe,
safe enough to be vulnerable, and know that
however warped his past or present may be,

That she'd choose to see the hope he
precariously clings to,
the hope he thinks no one else have confidence
in but him.

She'd like him to know and feel, that he's not
alone
and that, whatever that hope may bring,
they'll hold on to it, and firmly, together.

Roof

She climbs onto that roof again, that one unsafe
place where she felt safe.

The pedestal where she can look down on her
problems and briefly make believe
that she's above them and all the pointless chafe.

There, she felt peacefully isolated, from
everything she's incessantly been trying
to keep away from.

Even in the cold of the night, she finds solace
from laying underneath the dark sky
and knowing that not even the brightest star can
make her noticeable.

That only someone who's not deterred by the
danger of falling will try to climb up,
hopefully see her and will deserve to be the
company, that deep down,
she secretly wanted and has been waiting for.

The Child in Him

He just wanted to be out there,
to kick off his shoes and run
but inclined towards guarding the wall
that makes him feel like a man

A man who fears of being despised
if he falls down on his knees,
who covertly aches to be understood
by the world strives to please

A man who thirsts for the simplest things
and the security he's compelled to give,
he's just as scared of getting hurt,
something no one would believe

He wishes for someone to loosen the chains
suppressing him to be an open book
and masks how he feels deeply for things,
that you ought to have a second look

And see that he is no different
from that little girl inside of you,
who wants to feel special and appreciated
and longs for the kind love like you do

Behind his wall, he peeks out there
weary of being a man and no one knew,
he just wants to be seen and still be loved
by someone, by anyone, maybe by you

Her Truth

She's not crazy! She talks to herself often but
don't we all?

But what sets her apart from the common, is the
spirit she articulates when she
pretends to speak to the paper crowd.

She can convey nonsense, but she always choose
to have something significant to say.

That's when her heart speaks to her. That's when
her moments of pretend,
starts to speak volumes of her truth. It's
ingenious and just aesthetic,
how it draws a clear picture of what's inside her
heart

and I couldn't be any more proud of what it
shows
every
single
time.

Moving On

It's the time of "whenever" again
that suddenly questions where you are,
when you thought you've gone miles away
but only moved so little, so far

Unsure of what gets you back there
to the spot you're certain you left
again you rummaged in the dark
the last bits of courage that you kept

It's feel like a maze and you want to scream
you're desperate for a helping hand
with little progress you eagerly hope
you'd at least get to understand

How the time of whenever makes you itch
whilst you fight the urge to relive the hate
and dwell on your crushed dreams with the one
you believed was your soulmate

The world is round you remind yourself
Losses aren't always a loss
sometimes goodbyes, regrets and heartbreaks
is a rain for a good cause

The rain that will make clear the path

that your fate will soon take
the path that will gloriously lead
to the destined end where you wait

The rain that will produce a rainbow
that will make all things fresh
and will remind you, every brave step you take
only takes you to where you'll be blessed

Light in the dark

She unbearably pulled out all the daggers that
pierced deep through her,
she said "never again", then she falls for another
stranger.

Another stranger who will get lost in the
vastness of her beauty and truth.
And only those who are adventurous enough,
will be comfortable with getting lost in it,

And would brave his steps away from the path
leading to the door
and walk into the wilderness, into the
magnificently bright, unclouded fragments of
her

Past that margin where lies the part of her that
light doesn't reach,
the parts of her that she dreadfully wishes, won't
make you storm right out
but she hopes despite the gloominess,
you'll find tranquility in and choose to stay.

Ode to Dear God

Oh how thankful I am of your artistry
that exhibits the love you're surrounding me
with.

Your craftsmanship that I didn't realize,
I wasn't doing a very good job in seeing
or sit down on to appreciate and breathe.

And then your gift of words came pouring down
on me,
in each and every dead moments that I was
accustomed
to just let go by.

It blows strongly like a wind that cant be hushed
demanding to be felt but won't leave you
wondering why.

Oh how thankful I am to you dear God, that
now,
every one of it springs striking epiphany,

It's beautiful, my heart is full without a doubt.

That when I think back, it looked all but vague,

I was uncertain what to make of all of it,
but it unquestionably knows what to make of
me.
You know what to make of me.